The Effective DRE:
A Skills Development Series

Keeping Records and Budgets

BY RUTH BRADLEY AND
MARY ANN TAEGER

RICHARD REICHERT
SERIES EDITOR

NATIONAL CONFERENCE OF
CATECHETICAL LEADERSHIP

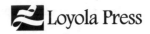

Loyola Press

**NATIONAL CONFERENCE OF
CATECHETICAL LEADERSHIP**

3021 Fourth Street, N.E.
Washington, D.C. 20017-1102
1-202-636-3826

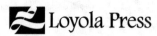 Loyola Press

3441 North Ashland Avenue
Chicago, Illinois 60657
1-800-621-1008

Acknowledgments:
Cover Design: Shar Coulson Design

ISBN: 0-8294-1060-0

98 99 00 01 02   5 4 3 2 1

Table of Contents

About This Series

The Effective DRE: A Skills Development Series has been developed by the National Conference of Catechetical Leadership (NCCL) to help DREs and those preparing to become DREs to acquire the basic competencies required to be effective in the ministry. We recognize that the term DRE will mean different things in different dioceses throughout the country. We use the term DRE here as broadly as possible and intend it to refer to anyone involved in or planning to become involved in a leadership capacity in a parish religious education program. The actual scope of the leadership position can range from responsibility for the total program to responsibility for a particular portion of it, such as the task of serving as the coordinator for a junior high or senior high program. Thus the booklets, though addressed specifically to DREs, are designed to be of assistance to all parish catechetical leaders regardless of the title assigned to them or the scope of their job description.

The material in the booklets is based on the *National Certification Standards for Professional Parish Directors of Religious Education,* a document developed by the NCCL and approved by the United States Catholic Conference Commission on Certification and Accreditation. The *Standards* document is quite extensive and identifies and explains a wide range of skill and knowledge areas. We did not attempt to cover all of them in these booklets. Instead we used two criteria in deciding what topics to develop.

First, we sought to identify some of the most essential skill/knowledge areas, namely those most needed by anyone in a catechetical leadership position (such as recruiting and training volunteers or developing a program). Second, we sought to identify topics where information is not as readily available. For example, topics like knowledge of Scripture, theology, or expertise in the areas of catechetical methodology and conscience formation, though clearly essential to any catechetical leader, are topics about which much has already been written. So we chose instead to offer help with other important but less frequently discussed topics (such as budgeting and keeping records or maintaining personal balance).

Authored by experienced DREs and religious education professionals, the booklets provide practical advice, proven methods, and specific procedures for carrying out the many essential tasks related to directing a parish religious education program.

The series can be used as a resource in a formal diocesan ministry training program or in a small group study program. It can also be used by an individual for self-study. The entire series provides a comprehensive study program. Or, since each booklet is self-contained, persons may study only those booklets dealing with the skills they wish to improve.

Finally, the booklets can be kept on the DRE's resource shelf to be referred to whenever help is needed in carrying out a particular task.

Introduction

Record keeping and budgeting are the nitty gritty of the DRE's ministry. They can hardly be considered glamorous tasks, yet they are necessary for ensuring the smooth operation of your overall program.

In this booklet, we have tried to identify the essential tasks related to record keeping and budgeting while providing proven, practical advice—including many sample forms and formulas—for carrying out those tasks. We hope these tips will help you avoid some of the common problems and pitfalls related to this aspect of our ministry.

Each parish program has its own unique needs. Job descriptions for DREs also vary from parish to parish. What is presented here should therefore be adapted by you to meet your own needs and circumstances.

If your parish provides you with an assistant, much of this work can be delegated to him or her. If your parish also provides access to a computer, many of the tasks can be handled in that way. It will still be your responsibility, however, to oversee these tasks, so it is critical that you are knowledgeable of what is needed and what is involved.

Finally, by law parish religious education programs are now obligated to follow many of the same legal procedures for dealing with minors that schools and other public institutions are required to follow. We have identified some of these procedures and provided appropriate forms. Since these procedures can vary from state to state, however, be sure to check with your parish's legal consultant regarding current requirements in your area. It is also recommended that you check with the diocesan office regarding normative forms for use in all religious education programs.

1 Keeping Records

INTRODUCTION

This chapter is addressed to an important part of the responsibilities of a parish DRE. Accuracy of the religious education office records helps the program run smoothly and efficiently. Keeping accurate records also helps save time and energy. The following pages highlight reasons for keeping each record. **Samples of each form may be found in Appendix II.** Each office is set up according to the personal preferences of the DRE and assistant. The key element in a smoothly operating program is the method of coordinating and retrieving student and family information easily, especially in the following areas:

- registration
- new registrations
- re-registration
- new student inquiries
- permanent family records
- medical situations and emergencies
- transfers
- attendance
- sacraments

REGISTRATION

This section will address two basic methods of keeping records: manual and computer. Many parishes have been able to take advantage of the modern age of technology and have all their records on computer.

However, whether a record is on computer or kept manually, it will be necessary for a family member or representative to complete a registration form of some sort. This form should include all pertinent information about the family so that any question can be answered by reference to one form or a computer screen. Sample forms are available for your use in Appendix II. (See Figures 1–3.) Because every parish has different needs these forms can and should be adapted accordingly.

When designing registration forms one needs to keep in mind the information that will be important and necessary for maximum office efficiency. Basic information includes:

- parish ID number
- parents' names (natural parents, stepparents, or guardians)
- marital status of parents
- religion of each parent or guardian
- with whom do children live
- address (indicate if parent lives with child)
- telephone numbers (home and work)
- emergency telephone number (friend or relative)
- child's *full* name (in case last name is different)
- child's birthdate
- baptismal information (taken from copy of certificate)
- dates and places of other sacraments received
- indicate any previous religious education
- grade in public school

- any learning disabilities
- any allergies and/or medication

Other information can be included, such as: other persons living in household with child; sacraments received by adult person in household; family parish registration status; language spoken in home; and address of separated parent who wants to be informed of parent meetings.

All of this information can help to give a better picture of the home environment from which each child comes. For instance, if there are other adults living in the household, can they be asked to help the youngster with getting to Mass, doing homework, or memorizing prayers? Knowing that the youngster lives with Mom but that Dad brings him or her to religion classes is a help when calling about absences.

NEW REGISTRATIONS

After the school year begins, few if any parish programs accept new students unless they are transferring from another parish program. Therefore *new* registrations are generally done starting in the late spring through the summer and into the fall. It is best to establish a *deadline* for accepting new registrations. One date that is convenient for many people is at the close of the third or fourth week of classes. Some parishes close registrations in early summer or the week preceding the first class day. Closing registrations in spring does not take into consideration families who are just moving into the area. Some allowance for new arrivals is important as a way of welcoming new parish members or a family that has chosen to begin their children's religious education.

The idea of closing registration and not allowing students to register during the year may seem untenable to some but doing so means one less frustration for the volunteer catechist. Sometimes, with open registration all year, a class might begin with 5 students, then grow to 12 students by Christmas, and then increase to about 25 students by April. Catechists are constantly having to review and reteach material to get the late arrivals up to where the class would like to be. Once it is established that there are no late registrations, parents have to make certain that their children are on time for class. Transfer students from another program, however, should be admitted throughout the year after you verify their attendance at the former parish.

Depending on your parish procedures, one of the first things for a new family to accomplish is to *register in the parish*. When the family arrives at the religious education office to place their children in the program, it is helpful if they can also be registered in the parish.

Have a packet of registration forms already prepared and available for families as they call or come into the office. This packet should consist of:

- a cover letter

- a copy of the parish policy that explains the registration procedures and requirements, such as baptismal information (Figure 4)

- the parish registration form

- the religious education program registration form

- the disaster information form (Figure 8)

- the medical consent form, if required by your parish (Figure 9)

- the volunteer form (if used)

- schedule of fees

- any other forms a particular parish program might need

This packet can then be mailed or handed to the family to be completed and returned to the office. It is often advantageous to include a return, self-addressed envelope to facilitate the quick return of the forms.

RE-REGISTRATION

Parents really appreciate not having to fill out registration forms each year. A permanent form could be shown to the family with any corrections added as needed. Here are some tips to help make the re-registration process flow smoothly:

- Re-register while classes are still in session. Once summer begins it is difficult, if not impossible, to get registrations completed. Most families are thinking about vacation, not next September's classes.

- Make registration easily accessible to parents either during class times or by mail.

- Ask for an address and home and work phone numbers *each* year when registering. Quite often parents move but fail to remember to notify the religious education office.

- Make room on the re-registration form for new students a family might want to register, e.g., a first grader, or even an older child who has dropped out of the program and now wants to return.

- Ask again for any *medical* and *emergency* information. This information *needs* to be current.

- Ask for any information not previously provided, e.g., baptismal information and/or first reconciliation and Eucharist date and place.

- Provide an incentive to parents by giving some type of discount for early re-registration.

Once the re-registration form has been returned to the office, the information needs to be checked against the former records for any changes.

NEW STUDENT INQUIRIES

Inquiries about the religious education program made by parents during the school year can be recorded (see Figure 4A for a sample form) so that they can receive a notice in the mail when registrations begin for the new school year. When inquiries are received during the year, you can:

- Record the parents' name, address, and home and/or work telephone numbers where they can be reached during the day.

- Determine how many children they wish to register and their grades for the *next* school year.

- Determine if the children have any prior religious education. This information is helpful in assigning the proper class.

- Inform the parent about fees, class times, and specific requirements necessary for registration.

- Also offer the parent a copy of the student text for the present year so the parent can be working with the child prior to enrollment for the next school year.

PERMANENT FAMILY RECORDS

Once a family has registered, a permanent family record form needs to be completed and filed or the information entered into a computer. Each year thereafter this family information only needs updating. The family member should check the permanent record for any corrections or additions. (Figures 5 and 6 are samples of possible forms.) Having permanent records speeds up the registration process, and parents appreciate not having to give the same information year after year. Also, with a form on file, baptismal information only has to be shown once.

MEDICAL SITUATIONS AND EMERGENCIES

The medical release and disaster information forms (Figures 7 and 8) should be duplicated, one copy for the office files and one copy kept with the catechist. If a disaster happens, emergency information is readily available. In the case of a disaster, the attendance form also should be taken with the catechist and students in order to more accurately do a head count. **When a designated person has appeared to pick up a child or children, do not release the child or children to that person without a picture identification.**

TRANSFERS

Should a student need to transfer to a different parish, as a courtesy a transfer information form should accompany the student. See Figure 10 for an example of information needing to be sent to the new parish.

ATTENDANCE

Standards for attendance should be explained in the registration packet that parents receive. Keeping good records of a student's attendance is important, especially in sacrament preparation classes and for students who must transfer to another parish during the school year. Forms for classroom attendance records need to be developed (see Figure 11). The form can be for an annual record or as a permanent record (see Figure 12) for the length of a student's involvement in the program. This record should be kept in the office, but the information can be recorded from class rosters on a weekly basis.

SACRAMENTS

The records of sacraments that each student receives should be kept in the religious education office. Additionally, any sacraments that students receive during attendance at the present program must be recorded in the parish office records. Also, as prescribed by Canon Law, information regarding the reception of confirmation needs to be sent back to the church of baptism. The registration form should have the baptism information for each student.

If an older child is planning to receive the sacrament of reconciliation for the first time, it is good to have the child or the parent tell the priest. Another approach is to use the card illustrated in Figure 13. This card should be filled out before the student receives the sacrament and then given to the DRE for record keeping.

PARENT COMMUNICATION

Parents like to know "what the schedule is." Keeping parents informed and involved is important to the success of any religious education program. Periodic letters from you to them keeping them "up to speed" are always appreciated. A handbook for parents also is a quick and efficient way to communicate information to them. It could include the following: schedules of classes and holidays, procedures and requirements for sacrament preparation, attendance, classroom and playground behavior, and discipline policy should standards not be met. If you have a dress code for students attending classes, it should also be explained in the handbook.

Newsletters that are sent home periodically are also a good way to remind parents of upcoming events.

Newsletters allow teachers to inform parents about upcoming projects for classroom activities and to recruit volunteers for those activities. Newsletters also provide a good opportunity to educate parents by having articles about the liturgical season, particularly during the seasons of Advent and Lent. For more information on newsletters, please see *Communicating Effectively*, another booklet in this series.

FOR REFLECTION:

1. Who among your present staff would you appoint to assist in the creation of parish forms?

2. In thinking about your parish program(s), what other forms or information do you need?

2 Personnel Records

INTRODUCTION

A religious education program is often heavily staffed by volunteers with possibly one or two paid personnel. Even though the staff is volunteer-based, accurate personnel records must be kept. It is a good idea to have a locked file cabinet for these records that is kept in the DRE's office.

Some DREs feel that this is just more paperwork, another way to keep the DRE in the office and away from the ministry. This kind of paperwork, however, *is* important and does not have to be done by the DRE. It can be done by the assistant or secretary.

The information on file can be helpful when another parish has asked for some specific dates, experience, performance history, etc. on a past volunteer. Recruiting new catechists is an ongoing task for the DRE. Periodically going through personnel files may reveal a catechist who took some time off two or three years ago and, with a little coaxing, might be ready to return. These files also may record significant milestones in a volunteer's personal life, such as a birthday or length of time as a volunteer. Acknowledging length-of-service anniversaries is important affirmation. Personnel files may also highlight specific talents that may be a good resource for the program.

While records of paid personnel should be on file in the business office of the parish, it would be advantageous for some information to also be on file in the religious education office. Automobile insurance information, driver's license information, and Social Security number should be on file for each volunteer and paid staff member.

VOLUNTEER INFORMATION

Detailed personnel records on volunteers could be a very rich source of information for a new DRE who comes to a parish and is not acquainted with the parish or its people. At least with these files, the new DRE can begin to become acquainted with the volunteers who work in the program.

A volunteer registration card with personal information should be completed at the time of hire (see Figure 14). This file needs to be updated each year. The following information should be included (or attached) on the form:

- name, address, telephone number
- birthdate (month and day only)
- marital status and number of children in the home
- number of years in the parish
- other parish activities or involvement
- other parishes of involvement during the past ten years
- grade taught
- awards won
- workshops attended
- copy of evaluation
- special interests and/or abilities

Having information on file for volunteers is a good practice. Sometimes just a telephone call to former parishes will provide the information that is needed. Some parishes have access to fingerprinting services at a reasonable cost. *Please note* that to keep fingerprints on file, the office needs to have a locked file cabinet and access to a shredder. Check with your state agency for more information.

PERFORMANCE EVALUATION

A performance evaluation should be given on an annual basis. If the person being evaluated is paid, it is important that this person have the opportunity to see how he or she is performing. For the volunteer it is not as necessary but is a very good way to say thank you for a job well done. Recruiting for the following year can also be done at this time.

Data that should be part of the performance evaluation includes:

- employment date
- position title
- type of review (i.e., annual, 90-day, special)
- supervisor name

Some factors to consider when rating an employee, whether he or she is a volunteer or paid staff member, can include the following:

- **Knowledge of position:** After one year in the position is the person performing at the expected level?

- **Quality and quantity of work:** Is the work accurate, neat, and of professional quality? Is the work finished in a timely fashion? Is all of the work needed being completed?

- **Initiative:** Can the person work on his or her own and when a task needs addressing, is it given attention? Is the person resourceful and effective in planning the work commitments?

- **Dependability:** Can this person be counted on when tasks and deadlines are present? Is attendance consistent?

- **Organization:** Does this person stick with projects and see them through to completion? Is there an awareness of deadlines and is timeline planning handled accordingly?

- **Communication skills:** Is this person cooperative, and is there effective communication with others on staff?

Strong areas of performance need to be highlighted. It is important to compliment and affirm these areas for each employee and volunteer. Also the person needs to know those areas that need improvement with suggestions as to what would be the minimum performance expectation. Together the supervisor and the employee need to plot a course of action with some specific steps to achieve some measurable outcomes for the next year. The written evaluation should be signed by both the supervisor and employee or volunteer. Space should be provided for the employee or volunteer to respond to the performance appraisal. Signed copies of the evaluation should be kept in the individual's file.

An ongoing evaluation is important for two reasons. First, it gives the person being evaluated some guidelines of expectations in regards to his or her job requirements and performance. An evaluation can be an affirmative tool in charting the growth of the individual in relationship to the job. It also gives the supervisor an opportunity to point out areas of weakness in a positive manner. Second, an evaluation is a valuable tool if a situation progresses to the point where it is necessary to terminate the employee or the volunteer. If performance has been consistently under par, and if there has been no sign of improvement, there is clearly justification for termination.

Remember, volunteers can be terminated if they are not fulfilling the requirements of the task they have been given. It may be suggested that this task does not seem to be suited to their particular talents. Hopefully, another position or ministry can be suggested for them to pursue.

On the positive side, an evaluation is indispensable when a promotion or advancement is available. Reviewing past evaluations can help in finding volunteers who might be ready to move into paid staff positions and in identifying staff members who are ready to move up.

Volunteers should be encouraged to take classes offered by the diocese in order to become certified catechists. The program and requirements vary, but basic certification can usually be accomplished in one year. Most parishes are willing to pay for classes upon completion of each class taken. This is to ensure that the volunteer will make the commitment and follow through. The volunteer is asked to pay at the time of enrollment and to receive reimbursement after the class is completed. This qualifies as an "ongoing education" budget item. Certification of paid staff members is a requirement in many parishes.

FOR REFLECTION:

1. In your experience what has been most effective for keeping track of personnel information? Who on your present staff could be responsible for birthday cards, anniversary cards, etc.?

2. How would you identify and encourage people on your staff who are ready for new challenges, such as further training, additional responsibility, and/or advancement?

3 Budgeting

INTRODUCTION

The second important area for a DRE is fiscal responsibility. The much-dreaded budget and budget implementation brings stress into the life of many DREs. For others it seems to be no more stressful than any other part of the responsibilities of the position. The following pages contain some ideas and hints that will make this part of the job less stressful.

Budgeting does not have to be an overwhelming task if the DRE knows what the responsibilities of the religious education office are in this area. A meeting with the pastor and finance chairperson and/or committee to establish areas of responsibility and guidelines for budget formation and departmental reports is essential if the financial part of the religious education office is to be handled accurately and efficiently. The secret is to schedule a specific time block to devote entirely to this task, collect all necessary records, and get it done.

Each DRE and secretary may have to develop their own budgeting forms and ways to report all financial transactions to the pastor and finance committee. In some cases these forms are set by the parish business administrator. An important factor in this endeavor is the ability to keep good records of how much is spent, where it is spent, and for what.

THE BUDGET

Financial planning and bookkeeping are approached differently in every parish. Some programs may draw funds directly from the parish while others have a separate checking account for program expenses with salaries and benefits subsidized by the parish. The budget is a tool that generates awareness on the part of the DRE regarding program expenses and needed income. It also helps the DRE to monitor expenditures and to plan the program accordingly. The key to a good budget is good data. The budget should be realistic, and a good beginning would be to examine the practicality of the previous year's budget in relation to actual expenditures.

Creating a budget is generally done on an annual basis and can be used to plan the next calendar year (January through December) or a fiscal year that parallels the school year (July of the current year through June of next year). The budget should be submitted to the pastor and/or finance committee and approval sought during the spring or fall. The entire budgeting process can be done on a computer. There are many budget programs available that include spreadsheets.

It is of value to the DRE to stick to a budget and keep financial records even if he or she is not required to do so by the pastor and/or the finance committee. If the DRE writes checks, accurate record keeping is essential. A monthly list of all expenditures plus a summary of these expenditures comparing them to the budget for the month is a sound business practice.

On the other hand, the DRE might have to request checks from the parish business office (see Figure 15). Good record keeping is still a must. If the parish only issues checks monthly, bimonthly, or weekly, be aware of check request deadlines. All check requests must be approved by and submitted through the DRE. Receipts must accompany check requests. Copies of all check requests, receipts, and bills should be filed in the religious education office.

The "Vendor" category on the check request form is used by some parish accountants. This is a number assigned to publishers, businesses, insurance companies, and individuals (e.g., Paulist Press, Smith Insurance Co., Susan B. Davis) who regularly receive payment from various parish departments.

"Chart of Accounts" is the universal account number assigned to a specific category (e.g., student insurance, textbooks, seminars, postage, office supplies, etc.).

The structure of budgeting varies depending on parish policy. The pastor may have a parish budget item called "Religious Education Department" that would include items such as payroll taxes, retirement, health and disability benefits, utilities, repairs and maintenance for classrooms and office space, and office equipment rental. The religious education program budget monitored by the DRE could include salaries and the above-named items, but this would be an exception rather than the norm.

Monthly allocations enable the parish accountant to be aware of the peak and valley months of each parish department. Generally, textbook costs, student insurance, and postage for mailings to teachers occur in October; hence, it is a peak month. January through March are generally valley months with another peak period in April or May with re-registration postage, sacrament costs, and an appreciation dinner or gifts.

Figure 16 is an example of a summary sheet for a proposed budget. The enrollment for this program is 1,700 students, preschool through high school.

Figure 17 is an example of a possible way to keep track of expenditures for those without a degree in bookkeeping or accounting. Most religious education program budgets would include the following:

- **Income:** registration fees, parish subsidies, fundraisers (optional), donations, adult program fees, and special fees for things like sacrament preparation and catechist formation programs.

- **Expenditures:** items such as salaries, gas mileage, telephone usage, and postage are often paid by the pastor but could be included in the religious education budget. Other items would be office or classroom supplies, student insurance, printing or copying, hospitality, training resources for workshops, in-services, religious education conferences, books and periodicals, audiovisual equipment, and program expenses such as speakers, handouts, a volunteer appreciation dinner, refunds, and general miscellaneous.

A budget item that needs to be discussed with the catechists is class rewards and prizes. A price range needs to be set for each. Items such as medals, holy cards, rosaries, stickers, small statues, and certificates can also be ordered in bulk with sizeable discounts possible. DREs can find local religious merchandise stores where additional discounts might be given.

Make sure volunteers are aware of the budget. A limit should be placed on the amount allowed for reimbursement. Encourage catechists to request materials well in advance for special crafts, activities, and prizes. A materials request form could be supplied to the catechist with a request that it be returned as soon as possible.

In some dioceses there are universal account item numbers used by all parishes in the diocese. If this is the practice it is necessary for the DRE to use these assigned numbers on the budget summary sheet, on the spreadsheet, and when writing checks or check requests.

BUDGET PRESENTATION

After the budget is drafted the next step for the DRE is to present it to the pastor and/or the finance committee. The DRE needs to be able to explain and defend proposed expenses. Some ideas to consider when presenting a proposed budget are:

- cost of living salary increases and raises earned through increased responsibility
- cost of increased marketing expenses (e.g., textbooks, shipping, postage, etc.)
- increase or decrease in enrollment, which is a reflection of parish growth or aging
- expansion of present program and/or creation of new ones
- change of textbooks that will necessitate additional expenses (teachers' manuals, testing materials, music cassettes, etc.)
- special conferences or conventions that may be a one-time expense. If travel is involved this category will be higher than normal in the budget. Don't forget to include a food allowance.
- repair and/or replacement of office equipment
- continuing need to update resources, especially in the area of media resources (videos, tapes, CDs, etc.)
- workshop fees for enrichment and further educational development of all catechists and paid coordinators
- the need to give paid staff an annual retreat as a means of spiritual growth

- hospitality for volunteers (as a "thank you" for service) that may take the form of an annual dinner, a day of prayer, or a family picnic
- programs with costs offset by fees or donations that need to be indicated in the budget both as expenses and as income

The major selling point will be to balance, without minimum deviation, the income and expenses. Critically analyze all item expenses and be able to *clearly* explain and support the need for each item. Be prepared for any area to be challenged and have figures ready to defend the need. Prior to presenting the budget, decide what is vital to the program and what is a frill so that compromises can be proposed to replace items that the committee wants to cut. Identify the most important needs and lesser needs. Here are some questions to ask:

- What items are needed to have an effective program?
- What items can be left off without serious consequences?
- What items can be put off until the following year?

There should be a meeting between the DRE, the pastor, and/or the plant manager to determine the items that will be on the religious education program budget. There is a budget category called "Furniture, Fixtures, and Equipment" (FFE). Does the religious education program budget need to reflect those items or will they be on the parish budget? This is one of the areas that needs clarification. The question of who has fiscal responsibility for maintaining the religious education office equipment needs attention. There may be other items for which financial responsibility is vague. Make certain these are identified and addressed.

ORDERING AND PURCHASING

The DRE should use numbered purchase orders (see Figure 18) to easily record and monitor expenses, supplies, books, and services. These forms can be purchased in an office supply store in either duplicate or triplicate styles. Include the vendor's name and address, the date issued, the order or catalog number of items ordered, and the universal account number under which the item falls. A short description of the item or services should also be written on the form. Keep a copy of the purchase order for office records. It will come in handy to match with the packing slip and invoice when the material arrives and also is a quick reference when putting together a financial report for the pastor or finance committee.

SMART SHOPPING

Be aware of early purchase incentives and discounts from publishers and supply companies. Offers of free shipping and handling are often given for ordering early. Also, if storage space is not a problem, further discounts can be available for shipping in the spring. Many vendors will agree to delay billing. Vendors also offer discounts for pre-paid orders or payment within a certain number of days after receiving the invoice.

Working with a textbook company's sales representative is better than working directly with the warehouse. The representative has the authority to offer discounts and can keep the DRE advised of current special offers. Most companies have 800 numbers for your convenience and savings. It is also a good idea to be familiar with your parish's policy and resources for volume buying or vendor discounts. Be honest with the sales representative about purchasing limitations. There are possible reduced costs that can be offered by a publisher. Also book vendors have displays at local and national conferences and are able to offer discounts for orders made at the conference.

Many parishes have accounts with local merchants who offer a discount. Find those supply stores that offer a discount to nonprofit organizations. Usually the stationery store is less of a bargain than the many discount stores that exist. Look through catalogs and compare prices as some offer better discounts. There are supply companies that service schools so connect with the school secretary for combined orders or for catalogs.

Supplies such as glue, construction paper, crayons, markers, poster board, and pencils can be purchased at craft stores, often at substantial savings. Again, talk with the school secretary, and combine orders when discounts are offered for larger orders. Look through the telephone book for school supply stores that often will offer a discount to nonprofit organizations or for large orders. Watch local newspapers for craft stores' end of season or promotional sales.

PETTY CASH

Petty cash is money set aside so that it is easily accessible for quick reimbursement or quick purchases without the need for a check request. It is not for large amount purchases nor should there be a large amount of money in this fund. Typically, a standard amount can range between $100 to $200. Accurate records must be kept of how the money has been spent. Figure 19 is a form that could be used to request petty cash. Figure 20 is a possible way in which petty cash records can be kept. The fund can be replenished as needed. Petty cash funds must be part of a budget. It will be necessary to see how much was spent in this area for the past one or two years and whether or not the amount was sufficient.

Catechists also like to have class parties to celebrate special holidays, events, or milestones. If refreshments are to be served, some sort of budget item needs to be added for this. Some parishes have parents volunteer to bring the refreshments, providing cookies, paper goods, and drinks. With this type of setup no budget item is needed.

HOSPITALITY

Because programs are heavily staffed by volunteers, it is important that a welcome and a "thank you" are extended to these important people. There are many ways in which this can be accomplished. At Christmas time a small gift such as poinsettias, candles, candy, or a tree ornament can be offered. Also important is the need for community building and celebration. An occasional meal together, an end-of-the-year dinner, a Christmas party, a potluck, or a family picnic are all effective ways to show appreciation and build community. All of these are budget items and need to be accounted for.

Staff days of prayer or a summer retreat opportunity are also ways of expressing appreciation and building spiritual strength for the staff. Both of these events are more successful if held away from the church grounds. It is also recommended that a facilitator or retreat director be hired from outside the parish so that the entire staff can participate in the event.

RESOURCES

There are many good magazines on the maket to which the religious education program may want to subscribe. Some of these include *Catechist, Religion Teacher's Journal,* and *Living Light.* These magazines offer interesting articles, ideas for classroom projects, helpful teaching hints, and thoughts for personal spiritual enrichment.

One for each catechist should be ordered if the budget permits or, if not, an affordable quantity should be made available in a resource center or in the religious education office.

National organizations such as the National Conference of Catechetical Leadership (NCCL) and the National Association of Parish Coordinators and Directors of Religious Education (NPCD) are also excellent resource opportunities for the DRE. When possible the DRE should attend the annual conferences offered by these organizations to discover good resource opportunities and to meet and talk with other DREs.

FUNDRAISING

Before any planning is started for fundraising, be sure to obtain the pastor's approval. Here are some ideas to make fundraising as successful as possible for special projects or general revenue:

- Identify the project and the purpose clearly.
- Determine the amount of involvement and accountability necessary for the project to be successful (e.g., teachers, students, or parents).
- Be aware of the responsibilities of controlling and accounting for fundraising items that students sell to the public (e.g., Holy Childhood stamps, candy, cards, etc.). Fundraising can become complicated and difficult to monitor because students only meet weekly. Other forms of fundraising (e.g., raffles, bake sales, car washes, etc.) might be considered. These activities require little or no initial monetary output.
- Plan some kind of accounting procedure in advance. Know who is responsible and how the

money will be collected, recorded, sent to the
bank, etc.

- Organize a system of recognition for sellers,
  contributors, and others involved who helped
  to make the project a success.

COLLECTION OF FEES

No child should be turned away because of a family's
inability to pay fees. No program, however, can exist without income. An arrangement made with the family pre-
serves the program's cash flow and allows the family some
assistance. Possible ways to work with the family include
arranging a payment schedule or waiving fees as a scholar-
ship designation. If specified by the pastor, deferred payment or waived fees must be approved by the DRE. When
fee amounts are determined they should reflect the culture
and socioeconomic circumstances of the parish. Keep in
mind that many parishes also collect an additional fee for
sacramental preparation booklets and materials.

The amount of fees paid varies according to local
parishes. Some parishes have just one fee per child while
others may have a family rate for three or more children
registering from the same family. Fees, budgets, and
planned expenditures should be reviewed with the pastor
or his associate for approval. Before meeting with him, *be
sure to have all your facts and figures prepared in advance.*

A system whereby parents are reminded when a payment is due should be established (see Figure 21). Also a
form/card should be developed that keeps accurate records
of when payments were received, amount, date, etc. One
that has been used successfully by several parishes for
these purposes is shown as Figure 22.

A year-end report showing all income and expenditures
should be submitted at the end of the fiscal year. The

spreadsheet found as Figure 17 could be used as a resource for this report. A report of the past year's program facts, growth, and activities with a projection of future growth and activities should be included along with the financial aspect of the religious education program.

FOR REFLECTION:

1. If all things were possible, what one thing or group of things would make your life more comfortable in the area of budgets?

2. Even though your way of keeping financial records may be good, think of a more creative possibility.

Conclusion

Record keeping and budgets are facts of life. Granted they are probably the least exciting areas of a DRE's responsibility, but if basic procedures are established, forms designed, and policy determined, these two areas become almost automatic. A DRE expends less and less energy as these responsibilities become part of the "ritual" of the religious education office.

Instead of putting off addressing these tasks, incorporate them into the regular routine of the office. Once comprehensive record keeping is established, it is a simple task to update or add to the files. If the budget is addressed monthly and records are kept current, the year-end budget report and next year's proposed budget become little more than entering figures with some thought given to adjustment for the coming year.

Record keeping and budgets should be addressed in an efficient and professional manner and then set aside in order to give full attention to the ministry. This will make a much more enjoyable balance in the daily life of the DRE.

Appendix 1
Computers and
Information
Management

Twenty-two parishes in the Diocese of Orange were contacted about their computer use. Nineteen of these parishes have computers and use them in a variety of ways. Three parishes do not have a computer because of a lack of money not a lack of desire.

Parish Data Systems (PDS) is the program used by 14 parishes with computers. Two parishes began with PDS and have since adapted to better fit their needs. The other approach is to find a programmer in your parish and have a system written to meet your specific needs for keeping records and budgets. Six parishes have done this. (Note: The PDS program designed for religious education tracks catechists, sacraments, and registrations for both families and individuals.)

A computer helps 14 parishes with registration and permanent records. Eleven parishes have attendance records in the computer, and 11 keep those records on cards in a card file. Two parishes keep current files only and each year wipe out the records and begin again.

Budget income and expense is an area successfully tracked on a computer. Five parishes have all their budget information on a computer, six do it by hand in a ledger, and six do nothing with the budget as it is handled in the rectory by the parish accountant. One parish keeps track of expenses on a computer even though the budget is the responsibility of the parish accountant.

If this survey were taken in any diocese across the United States it is quite possible that the results would be the same with a high percentage of offices using computers for record keeping and budgeting.

Note: To receive a free sample demo disk of the Parish Data Systems Program call Parish Data Systems, Inc. at 1-800-999-7148 or write to them at 14425 N. 19th Street, Phoenix, AZ 85023-6702.

Appendix II
Sample Forms

NB: Be sure to check with your diocesan office for normative forms to be used in all religious education programs.

Figure 1 Registration Form: Sample 1

INDIVIDUAL STUDENT REGISTRATION CARD (please print)

Family name _____ Parish ID #_____

Child's name _____ Birthdate_____

Address _____

City _____ Zip _____ Phone _____

Parents' names _____

School_____ Grade entering _____

LIST ANY SPECIAL NEEDS (for example, ADD, physical restrictions, medication, allergies)

_____

_____

SACRAMENTAL PREPARATION PROGRAM (Please list sacraments your child is receiving this year: baptism, first reconciliation, first Communion, confirmation)

_____

–side 1–

Please circle the time you would prefer your child to attend religious education:

Nursery: Sat. 5:00 p.m.   Sun. 7:30 a.m.   Sun. 9:00 a.m.   Sun. 11:00 a.m.

Ages thru kindergarten: Sun. 8:45 a.m.   Sun. 10:45 a.m.

Grades 1 - 5:   Tuesday   4:15–5:30 p.m.   6:00–7:15 p.m. or
                  Thursday   4:15–5:30 p.m.   7:00–8:15 p.m.

Middle school: Wednesday   7:00–8:15 p.m.

SACRAMENTS RECEIVED

	Date	Parish, City, and State
Baptism		
Reconciliation		
First Communion		
Confirmation		

PREVIOUS RELIGIOUS EDUCATION COMPLETED

Circle grades   N   PK   K   1   2   3   4   5   6   7   8   9   10   11   12

–side 2–

Figure 2 Registration Form: Sample 2

REGISTRATION FORM—RELIGIOUS EDUCATION PROGRAM

Date _____

Father's full name _____ Religion _____

Mother's maiden name _____ Religion _____

Address _____ Phone_____

Stepparent/Guardian's name _____ Religion _____

Address _____ Phone_____

Child resides with _____

Mail should be addressed to: _____

For office use only

Child's full name	Birthday	Age	Grade	Baptism	Communion	Penance	Year	Grade
_____				yes/no	yes/no	yes/no	_____	
_____				yes/no	yes/no	yes/no	_____	
_____				yes/no	yes/no	yes/no	_____	
_____				yes/no	yes/no	yes/no	_____	

NUMBER TO CALL IN CASE OF EMERGENCY (other than home phone)

Name_____ Relationship to child _____ Phone_____

–side 1–

- -

Please list all those persons living in your home _____

Name	Age	Relationship to child	Baptism	Communion	Penance	Confirmation
_____			yes/no	yes/no	yes/no	yes/no
_____			yes/no	yes/no	yes/no	yes/no
_____			yes/no	yes/no	yes/no	yes/no
_____			yes/no	yes/no	yes/no	yes/no

Do any of the children who are enrolling have a physical or learning difficulty?
yes ( ) no ( )

If yes, please give the name of the child and how we can help: _____

_____

Does this child attend special education classes in public school? yes ( ) no ( )

ELEMENTARY CLASS DAYS/TIMES (grades 1-6)
Sunday 8:30–9:45 a.m. _____
Monday 4:00–5:15 p.m. _____

Registration Fees:

$40.00 for 1 student _____
$60.00 for 2 students _____
$75.00 for 3 or more _____
Total fees _____

Additional Fees:

$15.00 for reconciliation/Communion
$10.00 for confirmation
$ 1.00 for disaster preparedness

Total registration fees: _____

_____
Parent/Guardian signature   Date

–side 2–

Figure 3 Registration Form: Sample 3

SAN FRANCISCO SOLANO PARISH
RELIGIOUS EDUCATION FAMILY REGISTRATION

Parish ID # _____

Family name _____ Phone _____

Address _____

City_____ Zip _____

Father's name _____ Work phone _____

Mother's name _____ Work phone _____

Children's names	Date of birth	Sex M/F	Baptism Yes/No

Previous parish attended _____

- -

(for office use only) Date parishioner left parish _____

Figure 4 Information to Include in a Registration Packet

SAN FRANCISCO SOLANO PARISH POLICY

• Regular attendance at Sunday Mass is expected.

• Appropriate behavior and common courtesy are presumed and expected at every grade level.

• Persistent behavior problems will result in the following response:

– Warning for disrupting class.

– Second incident, student will stay after class to talk to teacher.

– Third incident, student will be sent to talk to the coordinator.

– The next step involves the parent being called to accompany the student to class the following week, or a meeting will take place with the student, parent(s), and program administrators to discuss alternatives.

• After three unexcused absences, the student will be dropped from the class roster in order to make room for those on the waiting list. Students preparing for the sacraments will be required to make up the work missed during absences.

• Parents of students attending Catholic school will participate in the sacramental preparation programs with other parish families; students will participate in preparation activities for the sacraments.

• A child must be in his or her second year of Catholic education or religious education classes to be eligible for the sacraments of reconciliation and Eucharist. He or she must also attend Mass regularly.

• If your child is transferring from another program, please submit a letter from the previous parish, verifying what the student has completed in preparation for the sacraments.

• Students who have not been baptized are required to participate in religious education introductory classes, attend Mass regularly, and be part of the Rite of Christian Initiation of Adults adapted for children for a period of two years. Full initiation into the Church (baptism, Eucharist, confirmation) occurs at the Easter Vigil Mass on Holy Saturday.

• Older students (4th grade and above) who have not received the sacraments of reconciliation and Eucharist attend religious education introductory classes for two years and attend Mass regularly. During the second year, the parish will assist parents in preparing their children to receive these sacraments with other older students.

Figure 4A Inquiry Form

Date of inquiry _____

Parent name _____
           last name   first name

Address: _____
          street   city   zip

Home phone _____

Work phone _____

Emergency contact _____ Phone _____
                    name/relationship

Names of children to be registered	Age	Grade entering the next school year
_____	_____	_____
_____	_____	_____
_____	_____	_____
_____	_____	_____
_____	_____	_____

For each child, indicate level of prior religious education: _____

_____
_____
_____
_____
_____

Figure 5 Permanent Record: Sample 1

ST. PHILIP RELIGIOUS EDUCATION
PERMANENT RECORD CARD

Date _____

Name of student _____ Phone _____
                last name   first name   home

Address _____
          street   city   zip

Father's full name _____ Religion _____

Mother's maiden name _____ Religion _____

Emergency contact _____ Phone _____
            name/relationship

BAPTISM:
Child's name on certificate _____

Father's name _____ Mother's name _____

Church _____ Date _____

Address _____
          street   city/state   zip

RECONCILIATION: Church _____ Date _____

COMMUNION: Church _____ Date _____

CONFIRMATION: Church _____ Date _____

GRADES: 3 yr. 4 yr. 5 yr. – 1 2 3 4 5 6 7 8 9 10 11 12

Figure 6 Permanent Record: Sample 2

RELIGIOUS EDUCATION PROGRAM

_____
Student's last name

Address _____ Home phone _____
      street   city   zip   Work phone _____

Father _____ Religion _____

Mother (maiden) _____ Religion _____

Language spoken in home _____

Emergency information (other than home)

Name_____ Phone _____

For Office Use Only

Child's name _____ Yr. Grade Teacher
      last   first   middle   _____

Date of birth _____ Baptism date_____ _____

Church of baptism _____ _____

Address of church _____ _____

Child has received: Reconciliation ❑ Communion ❑ Confirmation ❑

*****List Additional Children on Back***** **–side 1–**

For Office Use Only

Child's name _____ Yr. Grade Teacher
      last   first   middle   _____

Date of birth _____ Baptism date_____ _____

Church of baptism _____ _____

Address of church _____ _____

Child has received: Reconciliation ❑ Communion ❑ Confirmation ❑

For Office Use Only

Child's name _____ Yr. Grade Teacher
      last   first   middle   _____

Date of birth _____ Baptism date_____ _____

Church of baptism _____ _____

Address of church _____ _____

Child has received: Reconciliation ❑ Communion ❑ Confirmation ❑ **–side 2–**

Figure 7 Medical Release Form

MEDICAL INFORMATION AND RELEASE FORM

Child's name _____

Physician's name and telephone _____

Please list any special medical information for your child (for example, any medications or special needs or education required) _____

_____

List any allergies _____

In the event of illness or injury, I do hereby consent to whatever x-ray examination, anesthetic, medical, surgical, dental diagnosis, or treatment and hospital care are considered necessary in the best judgment of the attending physician, surgeon, or dentist and performed by or under the supervision of a member of the medical staff of the hospital or facility furnishing medical or dental services.

I fully understand that students are to abide by all rules and regulations governing conduct and safety while attending religious education classes and related activities. Any violation of these rules and regulations may result in that individual being sent home.

_____
Signature of parent/guardian   Date   Date effective until

_____
Address   Telephone number

_____
Insurance carrier   Policy number

Figure 8 Disaster Information Form

MAJOR DISASTER INFORMATION

In the event of a major disaster, all students will remain at school until released to a **parent** or **other authorized person**.

Family name_____ Telephone _____

Names of Children in Parish Program:

_____ Grade _____ Date of birth _____

Medications (on regular basis) _____

_____

_____

_____ Grade _____ Date of birth _____

Medications (on regular basis) _____

_____

_____

_____ Grade _____ Date of birth _____

Medications (on regular basis) _____

_____

_____

Designated person(s) other than parent who may pick up children.

_____ Telephone _____

_____ Telephone _____

THESE RECORDS MUST REMAIN WITH THE TEACHER IN EACH CLASSROOM WHILE STUDENTS ARE IN A CLASS SETTING.

Figure 9 Medical Consent Form

AUTHORIZATION TO CONSENT TO TREATMENT OF MINOR

We (I), the undersigned, parent(s) of _____, a minor, do hereby authorize _____ as agent(s) for the undersigned to consent to any x-ray examination, anesthetic, medical or surgical diagnosis, or treatment and hospital care that is deemed advisable by, and is to be rendered under, the provisions of the Medicine Practice Act on the medical staff of _____ Hospital, whether such diagnosis or treatment is rendered at the office of a physician or said hospital.

I understand that this authorization is given in advance of any specific diagnosis, treatment, or hospital care being required but is given to provide authority and power on the part of our aforesaid agent(s) to give specific consent to any and all such diagnosis, treatment, or hospital care that the aforementioned physician in the exercise of his or her best judgment may deem advisable.

This authorization is given pursuant to the provisions of Section 25.8 of the Civil Code of California.

This authorization shall remain effective until _____ 19___ unless sooner revoked in writing delivered to said agent(s).

_____   _____
Dated   Father

_____   _____
Witness   Mother

_____   _____
Witness   Legal guardian

Figure 10 Transfer Form

NAME OF PARISH
Address
Telephone Number

To whom it may concern:

_____ has attended religious education classes at

_____ Parish from _____ to _____.

The last grade completed was _____.

His/Her attendance record is as follows _____.

The sacraments received are as follows:

     Baptism _____

     Reconciliation _____

     First Eucharist _____

     Confirmation requirements _____

_____

_____

_____

_____

_____

If further information is needed, please do not hesitate to contact this office.

Sincerely,

_____
     Director of Religious Education

Figure 11 Classroom Attendance Sheet

E – Absence   X – Present   U – Unexcused Absence

Date

Student name

Figure 12 Individual Permanent Attendance Record

Enrollment Date	Grade	Sept.	Oct.	Nov.	Dec.	Jan.	Feb.	March	April	May	Times Present

Remarks:

Figure 13 Reconciliation Card

> **PLEASE FILL IN
> YOUR CHILD'S NAME,
> TODAY'S DATE,
> AND
> HAVE YOUR CHILD
> PRESENT THE CARD TO
> THE DIRECTOR OF
> RELIGIOUS EDUCATION.**
>
> –side 1–

> _____
> *print child's name above*
>
> **is receiving the
> sacrament of
> reconciliation
> for the first time.**
>
> **Date** _____
>
> –side 2–

Figure 14 Volunteer Information Card

Name _____ Phone _____

Address _____

Marital status _____ Number of children in the home _____

Birthdate (month/day) _____

Years in parish _____

Other activities in which you are involved _____

_____

_____

Other parishes in which you were a volunteer during the past ten years

_____

_____

_____

Grade(s) taught _____

Awards won _____

Workshops attended _____

_____

Special interests/abilities _____

_____

Car insurance company and policy # _____

_____

Driver's license # _____ Exp. date _____

Social Security # _____

Figure 15 Check Request Form

SAN FRANCISCO SOLANO PARISH
CHECK REQUEST

Pay to: _____

             _____

             _____

             _____

Date: _____

Vendor: _____

Chart of
accounts #:   _____

Amount: _____

Requested by: _____

Figure 16 Budget Summary Sheet

Acct. Department	1996-97 Approved	1996-97 Actual	+ (-)	1997-98 Proposed	+ (-)
1341 Depart. Receipts	$49,000	$62,463	$14,113	$71,833	$ 9,370
1343 Refunds for Reg.	200				
1353 Returned checks	450				
Deposit Totals $48,350		$62,463	$14,113	$71,833	$ 9,370
Acct. Expenditures					
1158 FFE		$ 1,073	($ 1,073)	$15,000	$15,000
1420 Cont. Education				200	200
1421 Conf. & Seminars	750	833	(83)	800	50
1424 Food Supplies	150	26	124	50	(100)
1426 Auto Allowance					
1426 Rent-Facilities	6,750	6,000	750	4,375	(2,375)
1429 Equipment Rental					
1334 Office Supplies	300	1,127	(827)	1,000	700
1435 Postage & Shipping	1,000	671	329	800	(200)
1437 Other Supp. & Matls.	1,000	3,496	($2,496)	1,500	500
1438 Dues & Subscrips.	175	307	(132)	300	125
1440 Audiovisual Matls.	250	818	(568)	700	450
1441 Instructional Matls.	900	3,251	(2,351)	2,500	1,600
1446 Printing & Photocopying	800	1,475	(675)	1,500	700
1450 Licenses & Permits					
1475 Public Relations/Hosp.	3,200	4,123	(923)	4,000	800
1500 Repairs & Maintenance					
1505 Insurance-Students	1,300	927	373	1,100	(200)
1510 Textbooks, 1- 5	11,000	10,710	290	12,000	1,000
1511 Textbooks, 6-8	200	152	48	900	700
1512 Textbks.-Lectionary	6,600	4,246		4,300	
1513 Textbks.-P-School	500	868		900	
1514 Sacramental Prep.	4,400	4,399		5,900	
1515 Catechumenate/ Children	400	163	237	400	-0-
Dept. 400 TOTAL	$40,035	$44,675	($4,640)	$58,225	$5,450
Difference Income/Expenditures	+ $8,315	+ $17,788		+ $13,608	

Figure 17 Modified Budget Summary Sheet

SAN FRANCISCO SOLANO PARISH
JULY 1, 1996 THRU JUNE 30, 1997

UPDATED: 12-Jun-97
DEPT. 400 RELIGIOUS EDUCATION

ACCT.	DESCRIPTION	JUL 96	AUG 96	SEP 96	OCT 96	NOV 96	DEC 96	JAN 97	FEB 97	MAR 97	APR 97	MAY 97	JUN 97	TOTAL
1341	Department Receipts													
1343	Refunds for Reg. Withdrawal													
1353	Returned Checks													
1407	Salaries-Rel. Ed.													
1408	Contract Labor-Rel. Ed. Off.													
1415	Payroll Taxes													
1417	Retirement													
1418	Health & Disability													
1420	Cont. Education													
1421	Conferences & Seminars													
1424	Food Supplies													
1426	Auto Allowance													
1428	Rent-Facilities													
1429	Equipment Rental													
1434	Office Supplies													
1435	Postage & Shipping													
1437	Other Supp. & Matls.													
1438	Dues & Subscriptions													
1440	Audiovisual Matls.													
1441	Instructional Matls.													
1446	Printing & Photocopying													
1450	Licenses & Permits													
1475	Public Relations & Hosp.													
1500	Repairs & Maintenance													
1505	Insurance-Students													
1510	Textbooks–1 thru 6													
1511	Textbooks–6 thru 8													
1512	Textbooks–Lectionary													
1513	Textbooks–Preschool													
1514	Sacramental Prep.													
1515	Catechumenate/children													
	DEPT. 400 TOTAL	0	0	0	0	0	0	0	0	0	0	0	0	0

Figure 18 Purchase Order

56423

Vendor _____

Address _____

Amount $ _____

Explanation _____

_____

_____

_____

_____

_____

_____

_____

_____

_____

Signed _____ Date _____

Figure 19 Request for Petty Cash

PETTY CASH REQUEST

NAME: _____

DATE: _____   AMOUNT: _____

SPENT FOR: _____

_____

_____

CHARGE TO ACCOUNT #: _____

PROCESSED BY: _____

NOTE: PLEASE STAPLE RECEIPT OR BACKUP TO THIS REQUEST.

Figure 20 Petty Cash Records

PETTY CASH RECORDS

Date	Dept. #	Amount	Reason for request	Name

Figure 21 Billing Statement

STATEMENT

SAN FRANCISCO SOLANO RELIGIOUS EDUCATION

BILL TO:

Name _____ Date _____

Address _____

City/State/Zip _____ Parish ID # _____

Date	Type	Description	Amount	Payment	Balance

Please send copy of baptismal certificate _____

Please ask previous parish to send a letter stating religious
education completed _____

We need a volunteer form or $25.00 non-volunteer fee _____

✂ - - - - - - - - - - - Cut here and return - - - - - - - - - - -

Remittance _____

Parish ID # _____

Name _____

Date _____

Amount due _____

Amount enclosed _____

Figure 22 Payment Record Card

SAN FRANCISCO SOLANO RELIGIOUS EDUCATION
PAYMENT CARD

Family last name _____ ID # _____

Address _____

City _____ Zip _____

Parent's name _____

PAYMENT TYPE	DATE	CHECK #	AMOUNT	AMOUNT DUE

–side 1–

PAYMENT TYPE	DATE	CHECK #	AMOUNT	AMOUNT DUE

–side 2–

NOTES